How to Relate to Impossible People

DICK PURNELL

HARVEST HOUSE PUBLISHERS

EUGENE, OREGON

Cover by Dugan Design Group, Bloomington, Minnesota

Cover photos © iStockphoto

HOW TO RELATE TO IMPOSSIBLE PEOPLE
Copyright © 2009 by Dick Purnell
Published by Harvest House Publishers
Eugene, Oregon 97402
www.harvesthousepublishers.com

Library of Congress Cataloging-in-Publication Data

Purnell, Dick.
  How to relate to impossible people / Dick Purnell.
    p. cm.
  ISBN 978-0-7369-2367-5 (pbk.)
  1. Interpersonal conflict—Religious aspects—Christianity—Textbooks. 2. Interpersonal conflict—Biblical teaching. 3. Interpersonal relations—Religious aspects—Christianity—Textbooks. 4. Interpersonal relations—Biblical teaching. I. Title.
  BV4597.53.C58P87 2009
  248.4—dc22
                                                                                   2008030789

Printed in the United States of America

            09 10 11 12 13 14 15 16 17 / BP-NI / 10 9 8 7 6 5 4 3 2 1

To my wife, Paula.
I am so grateful you said on our wedding day,
"We shall be together until death do us part."
I love you more today than on that beautiful Sunday in 1982.
Together we are a team for life.

Contents

Do You Know an Impossible Person?

Most of us would agree that some people are difficult! They bother and irritate us. Personalities clash, straining relationships with family, coworkers, and friends. Negative folks, naysayers, and know-it-alls drag us down. And in any relationship, complete compatibility is a myth. Even our best friends or closest relatives sometimes misunderstand or annoy us. Tensions over the littlest things can worm their way into the closest friendships. All of us fit into the "impossible" category sometime for someone.

But some people seem to be especially obnoxious or arrogant. Their finger is always hovering over our "hot buttons." Their occupation is to spread malicious gossip about us or to create dissension and distrust. From those who sarcastically belittle or criticize us to those who are openly hostile, such are those who victimize us in ways that may bring anger or fear.

The easy way to deal with the variety of difficult people in our lives is to retaliate, either silently or in action. But God has not called us to the easy way. He desires for us to be ambassadors of reconciliation, just like Jesus, who reconciled us with God even while we were impossibly set on rejecting Him! Do you desire to follow Jesus, improve your relationships, and learn how to resolve some of those old conflicts? No person is impossible with the Lord, not even the most impossible one you know! He can transform personality clashes into harmonious cooperation, tension into respect, anger into peace. God wisely shows us when to endeavor to reconcile with people and when to avoid them.

The Bible is full of impossible people who were misunderstanding, arguing, fighting, whining, or mocking. None of us have experienced anything new to human interactions! God has more to say about dealing with people than about almost any other topic. He knows you and every person in your life, and He knows how you can relate to them in a way that honors Him and brings you satisfaction.

Just as He did with His people in the Bible, the Lord often uses impossible people to teach us a lot about ourselves and about how much we need Him. His Word is filled with examples and admonitions on how we are to interact with people who make our lives difficult.

But here is the really big question: Are *you* the impossible person?

Before we focus on the faults of others, we must look at our own. As I said, every one of us is an impossible person to someone sometime. This book is not really about the people who annoy us. It is all about us. We cannot fix other people. We can only change ourselves.

This 31-Day Experiment gives you an opportunity to deepen your love for the Lord and to learn what He wants to change about you and your relationships. You will study a different passage each day for a month and receive guidance in what to pray about with each daily topic. God will reveal to you how to think and what to do about specific people and situations.

Near the back of the book, you'll find a few pages titled "The Book of Proverbs on Relationships." It is a compilation of no-nonsense, practical bits of wisdom straight from God's Word and focused on how to relate to other people. If you want the basics on God's design for relationships, you can't do much better than this.

"Using This Book with a Group" gives you lots of ideas to make this topic a lively discussion for your small group or Sunday school class. Grow closer together and build up each other to revitalize your relationships according to God's Word.

By spending time each day with the Lord for 31 days, you will build a daily habit of meeting with God that could last a lifetime.

My Prayer

We are surrounded by a wide variety of people. Some bring out the best in us, and some the worst. With some individuals we feel confident enough to share our inner thoughts, but with others we hide our thoughts and emotions. Even with those we have known for many years, we often feel like strangers. We are forced to relate to some people even though we may not like them. They may include some of our relatives, coworkers, or neighbors. And some of our special, personal relationships bring us the deepest concerns. When we experience misunderstanding or stress with those closest to us, the hurt, pain, or isolation can be overwhelming.

Heavenly Father, I need you. I want my relationships to improve. You, Lord, are the Creator and Author of each life. You know everything about everybody, and I know that we all fit somehow into Your great plan for this world. You have made us for relationships. However, our sin and selfishness create all kinds of turmoil, quirky personalities, and suspicion.

I need Your wisdom and courage. Right now I am dealing with some impossible people, and I am concerned about what to do. Teach me how to build my relationships according to Your Word. Open my heart and eyes to everything that You want me to know and do. You are My Shepherd, so I trust You to guide me to develop satisfying relationships and to protect me from ones who could bring me harm.

Use this 31-day Experiment to change my life and relationships. I desire to love You more passionately and obey You more consistently. I ask all this, trusting in Your Son, the Lord Jesus Christ.

Signed _____

Date _____

My Covenant with God

I commit myself before You, Father, to do this 31-Day Experiment, *How to Relate to Impossible People*. Today, I make this covenant with you to do three things:

1. I will spend 20 to 30 minutes each day reading the Bible, praying, and writing out my thoughts and plans in this book.

2. I will ask at least one other person to pray daily for me that the experiment will change my life and relationships. I will ask that person if he or she wants to do the experiment along with me so we can share together what we are learning.

3. I will attend a church each week so I can learn more about You and how You want to change my life.

Signed _____

Date _____

How to Get the Most out of This Book

Preparation for Each Day

1. Obtain a translation of the Bible that is easy to read. If you want to use the same translation used in this book, look at the New International Version (NIV). Get a pen to jot down your thoughts, prayers, answers to prayer, and plans.

2. Pick a special time each day to spend time alone with your heavenly Father. Try to choose the same time each day— one that is best for you, when your heart is most receptive to meeting with God. This will help you to continue having a daily time with the Lord long after you have completed this experiment. The goal is to build a good habit that will last a lifetime.

3. Find a particular spot where you can clear your mind of distractions and focus your full attention on your relationship with God. Whenever you come to this place, you will anticipate meeting with the Lord.

Read (14 minutes)

1. Pray earnestly before you begin. Ask the Lord to teach you what He desires for you to learn.

2. Read the entire passage.

3. Read it again, looking for important statements that God impresses on your mind.

4. Answer the questions provided. Observe what God says about Himself and what He wants you to know about dealing with impossible people. As you discover more of His truth, you will understand much better how to live the way God wants you to live. Explain how you are going to apply the lessons you have learned to your life.

5. Choose a verse that is especially meaningful to you. Copy it onto a card and read it several times during the day. Put it on your computer desktop for the day. Every time you look at your computer, you will be reminded of the verse. Think about its meaning and impact on your life. Memorize it when you have free mental time, for example, when you are getting ready in the morning, while you are standing in line, taking a break, waiting for class to begin, going through your exercise routine, or walking somewhere.

Need (2 minutes)

1. Pray that the Lord will give you insight into your own life.

2. Decide what your most pressing personal need is that day. It may be the same as on previous days, or it may be a different one.

3. Write down your request. The more specific your request, the more specific the answer will be.

4. Earnestly pray each day for God's provision. As you progress through the experiment, exercise your developing faith. Trust God to bring peace to strained relationships.

5. When the Lord meets your need, record the date and how He did it. Periodically review God's wonderful provisions, and thank Him often for His faithfulness. This will greatly increase your faith and confidence in Him.

6. At the end of the 31 days, review all the answers to your prayers. Rejoice in God's goodness to you. Keep praying for the requests that still need answers.

Deed (2 minutes)

1. Pray for the Lord's guidance and wisdom to help another person during the day. Try to apply the particular passage you have just studied.

2. Take the initiative to reconcile a relationship. Seek to express God's wonderful love to someone who bothers you. Be a servant. Someone has said, "Behind every face, a drama is going on." Tap into people's dramas and share God's truth with them.

3. Ask others to pray for you as you endeavor to resolve conflicts.

Making It Personal (2 minutes)

1. Read the challenge for the day, especially the verses that amplify the day's topic.

2. Think about them periodically during the day.

3. Write down ideas about how you can put into practice specific lessons found in the passage.

At the End of Your Day

1. Read the passage again, looking for additional ideas about how to relate to impossible people.

2. Pray again for your need. Thank the Lord that He will answer in His way and in His time.

3. Record the deed God guided you to accomplish.

4. Review the Making It Personal ideas. Look for further biblical insights to help you apply the passage to your life.

Partners

Ask a friend or a group of friends to do the experiment with you. Look in the back of this book in the pages titled "Using This Book with a Group" for practical suggestions. Pray frequently for one another, that you will learn more about the Lord and how to live for Him. Encourage one another to be disciplined and faithful in spending time with the Lord each day. Share what you are learning.

Where to Start

~

Before beginning this experiment in relating to impossible people, take a few moments to evaluate where you are in your relationships. How do you feel about certain people in your life?

In order to see measurable progress in developing better relationships, decide what you want to see changed during the next 31 days. Specifically, what do you want God to do? What are the most significant things you expect from working in this book?

As you work and pray through this experiment, you may experience wonderful changes that come quickly. On the other hand, you may take longer—a month, six months, a year, or more. You might take three steps forward in your growth and then one step backward. But that is still progress. Don't get discouraged.

Keep moving. You will make progress as you are faithful to do the things God's Word reveals to you. Each small step of growth is success. Focus on these three areas to determine where you want to put your energies to reconcile strained relationships. Circle the suggested ideas below that appeal to you. Add your own specific goals.

Something to understand.
What would you like to figure out about specific relationships?

Write down your questions, and pray and seek God's will about them.

1. Why do some people bother me more than others?

2. How can I handle my anger or desire to get revenge?

3. What is the path to peace in some chaotic relationships?

4. How can I change the home or work environment to be more pleasant?

5. What contributes to my feelings of loneliness or discouragement?

6. How can I get along better with an important person in my life?

7. How can I encourage an underachiever or someone who always sees the negative side of circumstances?

My Goals: In the next 31 days of this experiment, I would like to understand…

Something to change.

Choose one or two difficult people in your life. What needs to be changed to bring harmony or at least a positive alternative to the present situation? You may want to start with one of these issues.

1. A bad attitude toward a know-it-all or a high-powered overachiever

2. Reactions to a person's obnoxious habits

3. Anger or hostility

4. Feeling like a failure when I am around someone who seems to have it all together

5. Emotional flare-ups when people criticize me unfairly or block my plans

6. Conflict or tension whenever I am with difficult people

7. Feeling rejected by someone I care for

My Goals: During the next month of meeting with God I would like to change…

Something to accomplish.

Write down what you would like to achieve during the next month.

1. Overcome a personality conflict with someone

2. Set a good example for someone

3. Reconcile a strained relationship

4. Forgive someone who has deeply hurt me

5. Decide what to do about a person who frightens or threatens me

6. Overcome being manipulated or smothered

7. Confront someone about a relationship problem

My Goals: As a result of discovering God's purposes for me, I would like to accomplish…

How to Relate to Impossible People

Part 1—The Kinds of People Who Can Make Your Life Difficult

Days 1–12

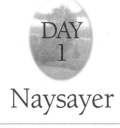

DAY 1

Naysayer

NUMBERS 13:26–14:9

After God miraculously brought the Israelites out of Egyptian slavery (Exodus 14), He instructed Moses to lead the people to the edge of the promised land of Canaan. Before they attempted to enter the land, Moses sent in spies to see what the area was like and what enemies they might encounter. Look at the spies' report about the beauty and challenges, including the Nephilim (fierce giants). The report caused chaos and dissention.

Read: Pray for faith to trust the Lord to help you to do whatever He guides you to do.

A. Describe the spies' report. What were the positive and negative aspects?

B. Why did the people gripe bitterly and burn with hatred toward Moses and Aaron?

C. Why did Caleb and Joshua respond differently?

Need: Pray for greater trust and confidence in the Lord.

My greatest need today is:

God answered my prayers _____ (date) in this way:

Deed: Put your trust in the almighty Lord instead of responding like the disgruntled Israelites.

Try to help people who see only the negative side of things. Point them to the awesome power of the Lord to conquer obstacles.

This is what the Lord led me to do:

*M*aking It Personal

Basing your decisions on what's right and possible is not always popular. Some people always look at the potential failure and express their reasons why "we cannot do that." As you depend on the Lord in tough situations, He loves to turn the impossible into the possible. God can change extremely harsh situations into places of victory. Don't let the naysayers demoralize you. Hang around people who build you up and motivate you to trust God for the impossible. Read what happened to Caleb (Numbers 14:24,30; Deuteronomy 1:34-36; Joshua 15:13-19; Judges 1:20). Faith has rewards for those who live expectantly.

DAY 2

Whiner

1 KINGS 19:1-18

Elijah lived during the time of wicked King Ahab of Israel and his infamous wife, Jezebel. They promoted the idol worship of Baal, which included child sacrifices. During a major confrontation with 500 prophets of Baal recorded in 1 Kings 18, Elijah called down fire from heaven. He miraculously defeated and destroyed all the false prophets, but his triumph turned to depression.

Read: Pray for courage to consistently trust the Lord.

A. Elijah had stood strong for the Lord to defeat the prophets of Baal. But Jezebel became enraged and angrily threatened to kill him. How did he respond?

B. Describe the interactions God has with His frightened and whining servant.

C. God did not display His presence in a powerful earthquake or a mighty wind, but in a soft voice. What is the significance of God's question, "What are you doing here?"

Need: Ask the Lord to pick you up from feeling down.

My greatest need today is:

God answered my prayers _____ (date) in this way:

Deed: Pray for those you know who are dealing with discouragement or depression.

Do something encouraging for a person who is struggling. Motivate him to face his difficulties with hope in the Lord.

This is what the Lord led me to do:

*M*aking It Personal

Are you discouraged or feeling defeated? Is your energy sapped, and do you want to run away? Is there someone you want to run away from? Turn to God for your energy and courage. Take refuge in the Lord, your rock and strength. Read Psalm 18 to discover how God saves those who trust in Him.

DAY
3

Dictator

NEHEMIAH 2:1-8

In 586 BC, the Babylonians, who had the most powerful army in the world, totally destroyed Jerusalem and deported most of the Hebrew people to cities throughout their vast kingdom. Then in 539 BC, the Medes and Persians destroyed the Babylonians. Around 445 BC, Nehemiah, a descendant of a deported Hebrew, was working as a cupbearer for the Persian king. Artaxerxes is known to have been brutal, ruling his huge empire with an iron fist. Nehemiah's job was to taste wine before the king to make sure it was not poisoned. Nehemiah had received word that the protective walls around Jerusalem still lay in ruins and that the remaining Jews were under constant threat of attack.

Read: Ask the Lord for a solution to a difficult relationship.

    A. Nehemiah prayed earnestly for three months (Nehemiah 1). Why was he afraid to tell the king about his deep grief for those living in Judah (Israel)?

B. How did King Artaxerxes respond?

C. How did Nehemiah present the solution to the problem?

Need: Pray that the gracious hand of God will be upon you.

My greatest need today is:

God solved the problem _____ (date) in this way:

Deed: Pray fervently for someone who needs help.

Ask God to guide you according to His perspective and plans. Look for ways to encourage someone else.

This is what the Lord led me to do:

*M*aking It Personal

The Lord can change the coldest heart and lighten the darkest relationship, as He did with King Artaxerxes. When you are in a position to help someone solve their problem, think about Proverbs 3:27-28. Anything come to your mind? Read also Jeremiah 29:11. Trust God to give you hope and a future.

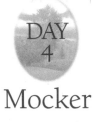

DAY 4

Mocker

NEHEMIAH 2:10-20

Nehemiah received permission, safe passage, and building supplies from King Artaxerxes to travel from Susa, the Persian capital, to Jerusalem. That is a journey of more than 1200 miles and would take Nehemiah and his entourage of soldiers and supplies at least three months. He was determined. But lying in wait in Jerusalem were several men who, not content with torn down walls, sought to tear down Nehemiah and the rest of God's people as they sought to rebuild the city and their lives.

Read: Pray for determination to get the job done.

A. The people living in the Jerusalem area were discouraged, depressed, and defenseless. They needed the city wall for protection and unity. How did Nehemiah motivate them to get started rebuilding?

B. Who were Sanballat and Tobiah? Why were they opposed to the wall getting rebuilt?

C. How did Nehemiah respond to their mockery and ridicule?

Need: Pray that the Lord will help you handle ridicule and mocking remarks.

My greatest need today is:

God answered my prayers _____ (date) in this way:

Deed: Pray to stand strong in the Lord's strength.

Ask the Lord to help you see past the hard exterior of people and view their need for Him.

This is what the Lord led me to do:

*M*aking It Personal

A familiar children's rhyme says: "Sticks and stones may break my bones, but words will never hurt me." That's wishful thinking—ridicule and mockery really do hurt. Read Proverbs 18:21 and Psalm 74:22-23. If you are living for the Lord, the ridicule you may receive is really directed at the Lord, whom you serve. Stand strong in His strength.

DAY 5

Troublemaker

NEHEMIAH 4:1-9

Nehemiah's ultimate goal was to help reestablish Israel as a nation. A strong wall around Jerusalem would give safety and community for the people to begin again. But Sanballat, Tobiah, and other enemies in surrounding countries vehemently opposed the construction. The last thing they wanted was a united, revitalized country that might threaten them. They were determined to stop it at all costs!

Read: Pray for the Lord's strength to keep on the right track.

A. Look at the tactics Sanballat used to try to stop the people from building. How did Nehemiah and the people respond?

B. Instead of responding with insults and attacks, Nehemiah chose a different reaction. Describe his tactic and the results it brought.

C. Why do you think the people worked so fervently?

Need: It is easy to get discouraged and quit when facing opposition. Pray for strength and peace.

My greatest need today is:

God answered my prayers_____ (date) in this way:

Deed: Pray for an opportunity to encourage someone today.

Some people hear taunts or accusations from others and get scared and give up. What can you do to motivate them to courageously do what is right and pleasing to God?

This is what the Lord led me to do:

$\mathcal{M}$aking It Personal

People handle criticism in different ways. You can profit from criticism by evaluating it to see if it contains any truth. It may give you insight into what would make you a better person. But when hostility or abuse come along, refuse to be discouraged. Know that the Lord is your strength. In Psalm 27:1-6 David explains what motivates him to face opposition. How can you apply his attitudes to your life?

DAY 6

Griper

NEHEMIAH 4:10-23

Sanballat and Tobiah had started out mocking and insulting workers, thinking they would never accomplish the impossible task of building a big wall around the entire city. But as the wall got higher and stronger, they spread their venom to other enemies of the Israelites. They recruited others to help foster a spirit of contention and griping among the people. These two became more devious and determined in their attacks.

Read: Pray for wisdom to know how to handle those who may dislike you.

    A. What rumors were circulating around Jerusalem?

    B. How did Nehemiah inspire the people to counteract these discouraging threats?

C. Write down Nehemiah's plan to handle the tough situation.

Need: Pray for wisdom to know how to respond to rumors and threats.

My greatest need today is:

God answered my prayers _____ (date) in this way:

Deed: Ask the Lord to open your eyes to people who are hurting. Seek a way to come alongside them to give them wisdom and insight into solving their problems.

This is what the Lord led me to do:

*M*aking *It Personal*

Rumors are difficult to stop, and they can cause great harm or pain. If others misrepresent you, counteract the lies with truth and compassion. Be wise in how you confront your accusers. Take the advice of David in Psalm 16 and take refuge in God.

DAY
7

Schemer

NEHEMIAH 6:1-9

The people kept working and building the wall. But Nehemiah encountered several new hurdles. Some of the people could not get along with each other. Dissention and arguments almost derailed the project, but Nehemiah boldly resolved them. Then more scheming messages arrived from Sanballat and his cohorts.

Read: Pray to keep focused on what the Lord has directed you to do.

A. What were Sanballat, Geshem, and the others trying to do?

B. How did Nehemiah respond to their messages?

C. Why is prayer so important?

Need: Ask the Lord to give you discernment to separate good ideas from deceptive ones.

My greatest need today is:

God answered my prayers _____ (date) in this way:

Deed: Seek the Lord and His truth.

Many people lack discernment and fall for unscrupulous plans that lead to negative results. When you see people who are going down the wrong path, try to warn them of potential difficulties.

This is what the Lord led me to do:

*M*aking It Personal

Some people give an honest critique or helpful suggestions. When you sense you can trust someone, build a friendship with that person. A trustworthy and faithful friend is rare. Proverbs 17:17 gives the characteristics of a true friend. Seek those people out as friends. Develop those characteristics yourself. Don't follow the directives of a deceitful person.

DAY 8

Deceiver

NEHEMIAH 6:10-19

⊷

The law of God states that only a priest was allowed to enter the Holy Place, a sacred room in the temple. So holy was this place that a priest had to wash himself in a ceremonial cleansing before he could even enter this room. Attached to it was a smaller room called the Holy of Holies, which contained the altar that symbolized the presence of God. Only the high priest could enter that room once a year. It would be the perfect hiding place from people seeking to kill you. But for anyone who was not a priest, to enter either room was considered a blasphemous act punishable by death.

Read: Pray for God's grace and protection.

A. Shemaiah was a fellow Jew and possibly an invalid confined to his house. Relate the advice this friend of Nehemiah gave to him.

B. Why did Nehemiah reject Shemaiah's plan?

C. What did Nehemiah find out about Shemaiah?

Need: Ask the Lord if there is any deception or hypocrisy in you.

My greatest need today is:

God answered my prayers _____ (date) in this way:

Deed: Pray for steadfast determination to do what is right.

Tactfully confront someone who is being two-faced or living two lives. Try to help him understand that honesty pleases God and people.

This is what the Lord led me to do:

*M*aking It Personal

Has someone close to you ever harmed you? Hypocrisy and betrayal shock us profoundly. When a good friend or close coworker turns on you or undercuts you, it can be devastating. But don't let it defeat you. Keep trusting the King of kings. Look at Nehemiah. He got the wall rebuilt in 52 days. Read David's responses to opposition in Psalm 3. His character and leadership remained intact despite strong opposition.

DAY 9

Plotter

GENESIS 37:12-36

Jacob, the grandson of Abraham, had 12 sons. But one of them was his favorite—Joseph. For a lot of reasons, Joseph's ten brothers hated him and plotted against him. Everyone has painful experiences in their past, and many have been victimized by conspirators. Jealousy and hatred make people do mean things. When you are the victim of lies and treachery, your natural reaction is to retaliate with aggression and hostility. But there is a better way.

Read: Pray to be set free from a bad attitude toward someone.

A. Jacob sent Joseph to get news about his brothers. But how did his brothers treat him?

B. One lie leads to other lies. What did the brothers tell their father, Jacob?

C. Read Genesis 50:15-26. At the end, how did Joseph treat his brothers?

Need: Pray for the right reaction to people who hurt you.

My greatest need today is:

God answered my prayers _____ (date) in this way:

Deed: Ask the Lord for sensitivity to the wounds of others.

Be a good listener. Ask people to share their stories and pray for them as you hear their pain.

This is what the Lord led me to do:

*M*aking It Personal

If you are the innocent victim of an evil person, you know the pain and scars that can last a lifetime. Getting rid of the hatred and the drive to get even is difficult. Evil people deserve to be punished. But if you harbor that hatred, you will become a hateful person. God is bigger than our pain. He can heal you and take the sting of revenge out of the memory. Even if you can get back at those who hurt you, choose Joseph's attitude instead: "You intended to harm me, but God intended it for good to accomplish what is now being done, the saving of many lives" (Genesis 50:20). Focus on the big picture of God's purposes. Read Romans 8:28-39.

DAY 10

Flirt

GENESIS 39

Joseph had 11 brothers who were jealous of him and hated him. When he visited them while they were grazing their sheep in a deserted area of Palestine, they ganged up on him and sold him to some traders as a slave. The traders took him to Egypt, where they sold him to Potiphar, captain of the guard for the Egyptian Pharaoh. Talk about being a victim and being lonely! Then things got worse. In Potiphar's house, Joseph was badgered by Potiphar's seductive wife.

Read: When you have been victimized, pray for God's favor.

  A. How did Joseph respond to his awful circumstances?

  B. Why did Potiphar trust him?

  C. When Potiphar's wife tempted him, what were the specific ways he responded? Why did he react like that?

Need: Ask the Lord for strong faith to reject seductive temptations.

My greatest need today is:

God answered my prayers _____ (date) in this way:

Deed: Pray for friends who are facing great temptations.

Look for ways to minister to those who are facing tough situations or are trying to overcome addictions. Get involved in their lives and assist them to get out of their awful situation.

This is what the Lord led me to do:

*M*aking It Personal

Joseph could have become an angry, vindictive man, sulking away in prison. But he chose differently. That is why "the Lord was with him." To resist temptation, you must have God's Word deep in your heart. Read Psalm 119:11. There is an old saying, "The Bible will keep you from sin, or sin will keep you from the Bible." Think about 1 Corinthians 10:13 and hold onto its message when you face strong temptation.

DAY 11

Bully

ACTS 26
(READ ALSO ACTS 9:1-30)

The Jews hated the apostle Paul and sought to kill him for preaching about Christ. They succeeded in getting the Romans to imprison him. At his trial before King Agrippa and Festus (the governor of Judea), Paul explained how he changed from a hateful persecutor of Christians to an enthusiastic proponent of faith in Christ. His powerful testimony could be called "From Murderer to Missionary" or "From Opponent to Proponent."

Read: Pray for courage to proclaim your faith in Christ.

A. How did Paul treat the followers of Christ?

B. What brought about the dramatic change in Paul?

C. How did King Agrippa and Governor Festus react to Paul's defense?

Need: Pray that Christ will greatly change you.

My greatest need today is:

God answered my prayers _____ (date) in this way:

Deed: How do you handle criticism and false accusations? Do you need Christ to change how you respond to people who antagonize you?

This is what the Lord led me to do:

*M*aking It Personal

Think of the most impossible person you know. Can you imagine that person coming to Christ and proclaiming the gospel fearlessly? You may say that would be a miracle as powerful as the resurrection of Christ. Well, Christ changed Paul, and He can do the same for that impossible person. Start praying for him or her to come to faith in Christ. Don't stop praying until it happens.

DAY 12

Traitor

LUKE 4:16-32

~

Jesus grew up in the little town of Nazareth in the district of Galilee. He lived there approximately 30 years before He started His public ministry. He returned to His hometown less than one year after leaving. News about His miracles and teaching quickly reached His family and friends. You would think that everyone would be happy to see the miracle worker come home, but this was *not* the case.

Read: Pray for sensitivity when you are with your loved ones.

A. In the synagogue, Jesus read Isaiah 61:1-2. How did He apply this passage to His life?

B. Jesus said that in Elijah and Elisha's time, God sent His messengers to Gentiles like the widow in Zarephath and Naaman, the Syrian general. Why did Jesus' hearers react so violently?

C. The people who watched Jesus grow up now tried to kill Him. But instead of getting discouraged and feeling rejected, what did Jesus do?

Need: Pray for inner strength and courage if you feel rejected or abandoned.

My greatest need today is:

God answered my prayers _____ (date) in this way:

Deed: Pray for those who have wounded you.

Ask the Lord to teach you lessons from your experiences. Look for others who are going through similar circumstances and reach out to comfort them with God's Word.

This is what the Lord led me to do:

*M*aking It Personal

Now you know the original source of the saying, "A prophet has no honor in his hometown." Often we expect our family and friends to understand us and accept us. But sometimes, instead of loving and encouraging us, they reject us and wound us deeply. Some people carry that pain all through their lives. Continue to try to build strong relationships with them. But if people are harmful to you, you may have to separate from them. Read Psalm 27:10, Isaiah 49:15-16, and Hebrews 13:5-6. Remember, the Lord is with you.

How to Relate to Impossible People

Part 2—Ideas for Relating to Impossible People

Days 13–31

Forgive and Set Free

Luke 17:1-10

Only once did the disciples ask Jesus for greater faith. Peter had asked Christ to allow him to walk on the water with Him, but he did not ask for faith (Matthew 14:22-33). The disciples did not ask for greater faith when He miraculously healed people, when he taught them about trusting God for something, or even when He told them to love God above all else. The only time that they asked Jesus for greater faith was in this passage.

Read: Pray for greater faith and trust in the Lord.

A. Jesus had just finished lambasting the Pharisees for their love of money, greed, and hard hearts (Luke 16). What did He now warn the disciples about?

B. Why did the disciples ask for greater faith?

C. What was the point of Jesus' analogy of the servant?

Need: Pray for great faith to forgive people when they ask you to.

My greatest need today is:

God answered my prayers _____ (date) in this way:

Deed: Pray to clear up any grudges or unforgiveness you have toward any people.

Some people hold a grudge for years and never let go. Share this passage with someone like that.

This is what the Lord led me to do:

Making It Personal

Granting forgiveness is a gracious act of kindness. You set a prisoner free from your emotional jail. As the old saying goes: "The longer you hold a grudge, the heavier it becomes." When you keep an account of all the wrongs people have done to you and harden your heart toward them, you become an angry, unforgiving, hard-hearted person. God has forgiven you without holding your sins against you—even when you return to Him many times to confess the same sin. The Lord wants you to do the same for other people.

DAY 14

Offer a Good Compromise

GENESIS 13

Abraham and his nephew Lot came from a foreign nation and settled in Canaan. They were herdsmen and had combined their possessions for economic development and protection. Both of them prospered over the years so that the land became too small for both of them. Trouble started to build as their employees began quarreling with each other. Harsh words and accusations flew. That region of Canaan simply didn't have enough room for these two large households. What to do?

Read: Ask the Lord to give you courage to try to solve a relationship problem.

A. What brought about the trouble between this uncle and his nephew?

B. Abraham came up with a big idea to solve the tense situation. Describe it.

C. How was the situation resolved?

Need: Pray for the people in your life and the tensions you may have with them.

My greatest need today is:

God answered my prayers _____ (date) in this way:

Deed: Pray for courage to try to heal any tensions or personality clashes.

This is what the Lord led me to do:

*M*aking It Personal

Abraham put himself and his future in God's hands. Lot selfishly chose the fertile land. What did Lot's choice really cost him? Read Genesis 14:1-16 and chapter 19. Seek some unselfish choices that may heal your strained relationship. List them.

Master Your Anger

GENESIS 4:1-16

⚜

Interpersonal conflicts and dysfunctional families started when Adam and Eve disobeyed God in the Garden of Eden (Genesis 3:16-20). They had two sons, Cain and Abel, who were born and raised away from Eden. They had different talents and skills—and a very different understanding of what pleased God. Cain believed the crops he grew would be an acceptable sacrifice to God. Abel believed he should give God the first and best that God had given him. Abel understood God's character much better. This created jealousy and anger in his brother Cain.

Read: Pray for power to master your anger.

    A. Both brothers offered sacrifices to God. But why was Cain angry toward Abel?

    B. The Lord sternly warned Cain about his anger. Describe Cain's response.

C. Cain tried to cover up the murder, but he could not hide it. How did God punish him?

Need: Pray to control your temper.

My greatest need today is:

God answered my prayers _____ (date) in this way:

Deed: Pray for someone who irritates or angers you.

Instead of getting upset and hostile, try to encourage and build up others.

This is what the Lord led me to do:

*M*aking It Personal

How should Cain have handled his emotions? No one makes you angry. People and situations reveal the anger that is already inside you. Who or what typically displays your anger? How can you handle your anger? Read a good Christian book on the topic. Read some Bible passages on anger. James 1:19-20 gives good advice.

DAY 16

Seek to Reconcile

MATTHEW 18:15-35

"Who is the greatest in the kingdom of heaven?" (Matthew 18:1). The disciples probably expected Jesus to point to a great king, a rich person, or a powerful politician. His answer? A little child. Humble. Trusting. So Christ taught us to discipline ourselves to become like that. But what about the person who irritates you? Or your obnoxious coworker? Or the one who criticizes you all the time? Humility seems risky. It can change all of your relationships.

Read: Pray for a childlike confidence in God.

    A. Suppose someone has wronged you. What do you do?

    B. And suppose this person changes his or her heart and asks you to forgive. What do you do then?

C. Suppose you don't want to forgive. How will God respond?

Need: Ask the Lord to open your heart to forgive.

My greatest need today is:

God answered my prayers_____ (date) in this way:

Deed: Pray for courage to forgive. Do what Christ commands. Find the person who has offended you and work to bring peace.

This is what the Lord led me to do:

$\mathcal{M}$aking It Personal

Jesus is not teaching here about dealing with personality clashes or different ways of doing things. The focus is on someone whose sin has directly affected you. The natural tendency is to nurse your hurt until you blow up, to gossip about how bad the person behaved, or to work on getting revenge. But Christ wants you to try to reconcile. Forgiveness is the heart of reconciliation. It is tough to seek it and to grant it. Both people need the humble spirit of a little child. Read Matthew 5:23-24.

Love the Unlovable

LUKE 6:27-38

The disciples knew that the Torah told them to love their neighbor (Leviticus 19:18). This was hard enough when it was directed toward their neighbor. But to love people who hate you? To love the Romans, who conquered them? To love the Pharisees, who were mean and deceitful? To love the tax collectors, who cheated them? This is radical stuff.

Read: Pray for God's power to love others His way.

  A. List the commands Jesus gives.

  B. Why follow these instructions?

  C. How does this passage affect you?

Need: Ask Christ to help you observe and obey His commands.

My greatest need today is:

God answered my prayers _____ (date) in this way:

Deed: Pray for God's power to put this passage into practice. Think how you can show kindness toward a seemingly impossible person. Regardless of their reaction, do something good for them.

This is what the Lord led me to do:

*M*aking It Personal

To love people who hate you does not mean you have to like them or enjoy being with them. To love means to seek the highest and best for someone. Christ died for us *and* for the religious leaders who hated Him and manipulated the Romans to kill Him (Romans 5:6-8). He did not try to get comfortable with them, but He offered truth and salvation to them. They rejected His offers many times. Their actions and hostility drove Him away from them (Mark 3:1-6). They bore the consequences. You are not responsible for other peoples' attitudes and actions, just your own. Seek to love them.

DAY 18

Examine Your Heart First

LUKE 6:39-49

Christ had just explained how a disciple of His thinks and lives. Upon hearing such things, we can be tempted to make ourselves feel better by focusing on and bringing attention to the shortcomings of others. "Well, I'm not like that person!" Another option is to fake it—to look good on the outside but choose disobedience on the inside. Obviously neither attitude is an option for a wholehearted disciple of Jesus Christ.

Read: Ask the Lord to make you a forgiver and a giver.

A. Why look at the plank of wood in your own eye first?

B. What does your speech reveal?

C. Describe the difference between a person who obeys Christ and one who does not.

Need: Pray that the Lord would reveal anything in your life that displeases Him.

My greatest need today is:

God answered my prayers_____ (date) in this way:

Deed: Pray to bear good fruit. Help someone else achieve their goals. Go the extra mile to reinforce godly attitudes and behavior.

This is what the Lord led me to do:

*M*aking It Personal

Change your heart to change your behavior. Read Matthew 7:3-5. That which is in your heart will eventually come out of your mouth. So what has your mouth been telling you (and others) about your heart? People don't make you be-little someone. They only reveal what is already in your heart. People don't make you lie, lust, or lash out. Those things are already inside you. How can you change your heart? That is the major question. Read Psalm 139:23-24 and Psalm 51.

Keep Praying

LUKE 18:1-8

Parables paint a vivid, simple story of a complex thought or concept. People who really wanted to know more about God received insight into the meaning Christ conveyed. But for those who rejected the Lord, the meaning was a mystery. Christ had just healed ten lepers—a miracle that set people talking. Then He taught authoritatively about the coming of the kingdom of God in a way no one else had ever done. After these amazing yet mysterious things, He told a parable. He wanted His disciples to get their minds around something very significant.

Read: Pray Christ will open your mind and heart about this parable.

A. Jesus rarely gave the main point of His parable. But He does here. What is it?

B. Because the woman in the parable had no husband to help her, she sought the help of the judge. Why did the judge finally answer her request?

C. What did Christ want His disciples to learn from the parable?

Need: Ask the Lord to help you consistently and fervently pray about your problem.

My greatest need today is:

God answered my prayers _____ (date) in this way:

Deed: Pray for someone who is going through a difficult time. Listen to their plight and pray with them for a resolution. Keep praying about it until the Lord answers.

This is what the Lord led me to do:

*M*aking It Personal

When we have problems with people, the simplest reaction is to talk negatively about them to others or to get angry. Have you ever tried to assemble a toy or electronic gadget, only to be reminded of the old saying, "When all else fails, read the directions"? We have that same attitude spiritually when we are facing a difficulty. "When all else fails, pray." Yet Christ emphasizes the opposite: pray, pray more, keep praying, don't quit, pray until God answers. That shows your faith. Read Philippians 4:6-7.

DAY 20

Agree to Disagree

ACTS 15:22-41

Barnabas and Paul were as close as brothers. On Paul's first missionary journey, they traveled together, spreading the gospel of Christ throughout the Mediterranean area and Greece (Acts 13–14). For part of that time, Barnabas' young cousin Mark traveled with them. During the trip, the missionary team was severely persecuted. Mark apparently got scared and abandoned them. This created tension between the two leaders.

Read: Pray for harmony in your relationships.

A. When Paul and Barnabas were planning a second missionary journey, what issue did they have a sharp disagreement about?

B. How did they resolve it?

C. Years later, near the end of his life, what did Paul say about Mark? (See 2 Timothy 4:11.)

Need: Pray to hold to your convictions, but be humble when you are wrong.

My greatest need today is:

God answered my prayers _____ (date) in this way:

Deed: Try to repair a friendship that has been strained or broken.

Be the peacemaker. Look for opportunities to build your companionship.

This is what the Lord led me to do:

*M*aking It Personal

Life would be boring if we all thought alike. Good friends can disagree and stay friendly. Sometimes you have to go your separate ways. However, avoid becoming a divisive trouble-maker. Leave room for God to work in your lives in different ways. Encourage each other to follow Christ faithfully (Hebrews 10:24-25). Remember, even good Christian friends can agree to disagree on different issues. As Christians have said since the seventeenth century, "In essentials unity, in non-essentials liberty, in all things charity."*

* Paul eventually was impressed by and reconciled to Mark but not to his mentor, Barnabas. I wonder why. Barnabas had a sterling reputation in the Christian community and went out of his way to befriend Saul and then go to Tarsus to bring Saul into the ministry (Acts 9–11). Why didn't Paul make an effort to be reconciled with him? Perhaps Barnabas, who was older, died not long after, and the matter was closed before feelings could calm down and a reconciliation could take place. And perhaps Paul's approval and value of Mark also included an unspoken repayment of kindness through Mark to Barnabas.

DAY 21

Give Your Anger to God

ROMANS 12:9-21

The believers in Rome during the time of Paul (around 60 AD) were persecuted by Nero. Many were wrapped in the hides of wild beasts and torn to pieces by dogs or hung on crosses and burned alive to illumine the night. They were misunderstood, ostracized, and afflicted. Yet Paul admonished them to behave in an entirely different manner than the pagans did.

Read: Pray to be at peace with people who trouble you.

A. List all the commands in this passage. What do they say about how to behave?

B. How are Christ followers supposed to treat people who wrong them?

C. How does God want you to handle your anger?

Need: Pray for the strength to obey God's commands.

My greatest need today is:

God answered my prayers_____ (date) in this way:

Deed: Check your motives. Pray for the strength to love without being hypocritical. If you have violated any of these admonitions, confess them to God and, if appropriate, to the people you have affected. Seek to live at peace with them.

This is what the Lord led me to do:

Making It Personal

Hurt people hurt people. Instead of desiring to get revenge when you are hurt by someone, give your pain to God. He is the righteous Judge. Let Him take care of the punishment. Focus on love, harmony, and peace. This attitude frees you to pray for your attackers that they would respond to the Lord and stop hurting you and other people. What do you need to change to behave like that?

DAY 22

Live by the Spirit

GALATIANS 5:13-23

The people in the church in Galatia believed in Christ, but they struggled with holding on to rules and practices from their pre-Christian days. They listened to false teachers and agitators who said the Galatians had to obey legalistic rituals. Their confusion about the basics of Christian living produced bickering and dissention. Sounds like a church full of impossible people! How could they get along?

Read: Pray to obey the truth.

A. Why are our sinful nature and the Holy Spirit in conflict with each other?

B. If you live according to your sinful nature and its desires, how will you behave?

C. If you live by the power of the Holy Spirit, what will He produce in your life?

Need: Pray to crucify your sinful desires and to live by the Holy Spirit.

My greatest need today is:

God answered my prayers _____ (date) in this way:

Deed: Pray to live by the Holy Spirit.* Think about the impossible people in your life. Seek a way to trust the Holy Spirit to respond to them with the fruit that only He can produce in you.

This is what the Lord led me to do:

$\mathcal{M}$aking It Personal

Christ sets us free so we will choose to obey God's Word. Obeying God is not confining or limiting. Actually, He gives you the power to reject the pressures and temptations of the old sinful nature. The power of the Holy Spirit and the fruit He produces changes relationships. To see the struggle between the old self and the new self in a slightly different way, read Romans 7–8.

* To understand more about the Holy Spirit, visit www.transferableconcepts.org and click on "Be filled with the Holy Spirit" by Bill Bright.

DAY 23

Accept the Differences

EPHESIANS 4:1-16

Diversity is prized by God, but not always by His people. Paul wrote from a Roman prison, telling believers to learn to build unity. That doesn't mean that everyone must be alike—that's uniformity. Just as an orchestra contains a wide variety of instruments playing different notes to bring rich harmony, so differences bring richness to our lives. Could you imagine everyone being the same? Snore.

Read: Pray to appreciate the differences in people.

A. What qualities in your character does God want you to develop?

B. What do you have in common with other Christians?

C. Why did Christ give a variety of gifts, and how have you seen this work practically?

Need: Pray to identify and develop whatever gifts God has given to you.

My greatest need today is:

God answered my prayers _____ (date) in this way:

Deed: Pray to understand how your gifts fit with other Christians' and how their gifts fit with yours. Instead of dwelling on the irritations you experience with others, look for the things you have in common. Build harmonious relationships with them.

This is what the Lord led me to do:

$\mathcal{M}$aking It Personal

We can get irritated not only by differences but also by similarities. If you are loud and controlling, you may dislike someone who is loud and controlling. If you procrastinate, you may not like other procrastinators. As Christians you have the same Lord, the same heavenly Father, and the same Holy Spirit who lives inside you. Regardless of whether your personalities or mannerisms are opposite or similar, dwell on loving one another as Christ commanded. Read John 17:20-23.

DAY 24

Imitate God

EPHESIANS 4:17–5:2

We learn how to behave by observing people around us. We are easily influenced by and can become like those we spend time with. When you get right down to it, underneath the surface and deep in our hearts, either self or Christ controls us. We have choices to make that determine our character and behavior. Whom you choose to guide your life makes a huge impact on how you behave. We must choose wisely, for our decision will lead to consequences.

Read: Pray to be willing to follow the Lord regardless of those around you.

A. Those who don't know Christ tend to rationalize their actions and attitudes. How does Paul describe these people?

B. When you put on the new self, which is created to be like God, how will you live differently?

C. As you imitate God, how will you treat other people?

Need: Pray to be kind, compassionate, and forgiving.

My greatest need today is:

God answered my prayers _____ (date) in this way:

Deed: The model for life is God Himself. Thank God that Christ showed us how to live.

What do you need to change to reflect God's character? Demonstrate to a few people that you love them.

This is what the Lord led me to do:

*M*aking It Personal

You will become more like God as you try to imitate Him. When you trusted Christ for salvation, the Holy Spirit gave you new life and new focus. This is why Paul writes forcefully, "Be imitators of God." The more you focus on God and how He treats people, the more you will do those same things. Read 1 Corinthians 11:1. Follow the people who are focusing on God.

Date _____

DAY 25

Identify Your True Enemy

EPHESIANS 6:10-18

Paul was victimized and tossed into a Roman prison on false charges when he wrote this. Who was his enemy? A guard? Nero? The Jewish religious leaders who lied about him? He said no. Who is your real enemy? Your spouse? A roommate? A parent? A coworker? Your boss? An employee? A neighbor? Paul would say, "Think again."

Read: Ask Christ to clarify your thinking about the source of your real opposition.

A. "Flesh and blood" (Ephesians 6:12) refers to people. Is a person your real enemy? Who is?

B. List all the commands in this passage. What does the Lord want you to do?

C. What is each piece in the armor of God? What is its purpose?

Need: Pray to put on the full armor of God each day.

My greatest need today is:

God answered my prayers _____ (date) in this way:

Deed: Ask the Lord to help you look beyond the human difficulty to see the real battle.

Focus on one part of the armor of God and use it today. This is what the Lord led me to do:

*M*aking It Personal

Your real enemy is Satan. His whole scheme is to destroy you and any good relationships that you have. What is the solution to defeat Satan's schemes? It's the armor of God. He is the only one that can defeat the devil (1 John 4:4). Daily use each part of the armor that God gave you to defeat Satan. Build fulfilling relationships and heal broken ones.

DAY
26

Transform Difficulties into Opportunities

Philippians 1:12-30

As Paul looked at damp Roman prison walls waiting to find out if Nero would kill him or let him go, he wrote to the people in the city of Philippi. They enjoyed freedom while he was guarded day and night by the elite palace prison guards. Depression and despair would be normal for a person living in those horrible circumstances. But Paul steadfastly trusted God and enthusiastically shared the good news of Christ with everyone who would listen—even the guards. Amazing things happened.

Read: Pray for a joyful attitude even in tough times.

A. Why did Paul consider his imprisonment an advancement for the gospel?

B. Instead of fighting imprisonment, what was Paul's struggle?

C. How does Paul want us to conduct ourselves?

Need: Ask Christ to change your attitude about stressful relationships or difficult circumstances.

My greatest need today is:

God answered my prayers _____ (date) in this way:

Deed: The Philippians helped Paul by praying earnestly for him. Pray the same way for others in need.

What kind things can you do today for someone in a tough situation?

This is what the Lord led me to do:

*M*aking It Personal

Most people imprisoned on false charges waiting for a decision from an irrational man like Nero would be depressed or fearful, hoping and pleading for release. Not Paul! He saw his extreme situation as an opportunity to spread the gospel of salvation. He was chained to guards for hours. Can you imagine being chained to the apostle Paul? No wonder many of them came to faith in Christ. Think of how you can change a tough situation into an advancement for the gospel. Read Acts 16:11-40 to learn how the church at Philippi got started through a faithful businesswoman.

Date _____

DAY 27

Set Your Heart and Mind on Things Above

COLOSSIANS 3:1-11

Impossible people—Paul was surrounded by them. His situation was probably far worse than anything you may encounter. Yet he advises the people living in freedom in Colosse how to solve their relationship problems. He doesn't complain about his dire situation, but tries to motivate the Colossians to live together in harmony. He writes (in effect), "God says get a life—a new one."

Read: Pray for a radical determination to live a godly life.

A. Why can you set your heart and mind on things above?

B. You were crucified with Christ, so you should consider yourself dead and unresponsive to what things?

C. Now that you have been raised with Christ, how are you being renewed?

Need: Ask Christ to bring out His character in your life.

My greatest need today is:

God answered my prayers _____ (date) in this way:

Deed: Pray that you will put on the new self every day. Even if you are around people who are dead spiritually, you can live life as the alive new creation that you are!

This is what the Lord led me to do:

*M*aking It Personal

Contrast your old self and your new self. The old self was self-centered, seethed angrily under the surface, destructively criticized others, and acted selfishly with a "me first" attitude. Because Christ now lives in you, you are new inside. Whenever the old attitudes and temptations come up, say, "That old self is now dead. My new self is focused on entirely different things." Show you have been raised from the dead! Read 2 Corinthians 5:17.

DAY 28

Resolve Conflicts

COLOSSIANS 3:12–4:1

When you get frustrated with people who become roadblocks to your happiness, you may naturally blame those individuals for your anguish. You might be tempted to get back at them, to show them up, to dig at their weaknesses, to trade sarcasm for sarcasm. The trouble is that when you react like that, you become just like them. No one can tell the difference. Consequently, you need to change. So here they are—tips for getting along with impossible people.

Read: Pray to see God's ultimate goal for your relationships.

    A. God says you are chosen, holy, and dearly loved. What actions would reveal your new nature?

    B. If the peace of Christ and the words of Christ fill your heart and mind, what will you do?

    C. How can family relationships and work activities reveal your goal to do all in the name of Jesus?

Need: Ask the Lord Jesus to help you please Him.

My greatest need today is:

God answered my prayers _____ (date) in this way:

Deed: Pray for wisdom about a complex relationship.

Try to turn a strained relationship into a peaceful one.
This is what the Lord led me to do:

$\mathcal{M}$aking It Personal

You may be tempted to erroneously think, *God is too busy to listen to the little concerns that bother me.* Wrong! God is interested in every part of your life. Bring Him into every relationship so that people will see you are serving Christ. He cares about everything about you. Read 1 Peter 5:6-7.

DAY 29

Base Your Life on the Truth

2 TIMOTHY 3

This is the next to last chapter of the last letter Paul wrote. He was writing from a Roman dungeon, chained up as a criminal on death row. According to tradition, he was beheaded by Nero soon after he wrote 2 Timothy. In his farewell letter, Paul instructed Timothy, whom he considered like a son, to remain true to Christ and God's Word regardless of what situations he faced.

Read: Pray for self-discipline to follow God's Word every day.

A. Describe the characteristics of people who do not have God in their lives.

B. What did Timothy learn from Paul's life?

C. Why will people who live for Christ probably face persecution?

Need: Ask the Lord to teach you more from His holy Scriptures, and listen to the Holy Spirit.

My greatest need today is:

God answered my prayers_____ (date) in this way:

Deed: Pray for a few people who need to base their lives on the solid foundation of God's Word. Expect the Lord to give you an opportunity to share with them what you are learning.

This is what the Lord led me to do:

*M*aking It Personal

God's Word can teach, rebuke, correct, and train you in righteousness. That's why it is so critical to study it, memorize passages, and share what you are learning with others. The more you internalize God's instructions for life, the more consistently you will live it. Others may ostracize you, taunt you, or try to drag you down. But hold on to what you know is the truth. Read Psalm 119.

DAY 30

Control Your Tongue

JAMES 3

James is passionate about people following the Lord whole-heartedly. Hypocrisy and deceit have no place in the lives of Christ followers. The gospel is worth living to the core of your being. Why be fake? None of us can claim perfection, but we can admit our sin and ask God for the power to change—and He will give us that power! Humbly put your faith into action. That is the core of the Christian life. Now, if we can only get our tongues to follow along!

Read: Pray for power over your tongue.

    A. James uses three illustrations to show how the tongue compares to the rest of your body. Explain them.

    B. The tongue is a small part of your body, but it causes big problems. Describe the characteristics of an untamed tongue.

    C. Compare the wisdom of the world with the wisdom that comes from above.

Need: Pray to tame your tongue and to speak the wisdom that only God gives.

My greatest need today is:

God answered my prayers _____ (date) in this way:

Deed: Seek God's wisdom to be a peacemaker, not a trouble-maker. Your tongue can build people up or tear them down. It can be critical, destructive, and cantankerous. Work on bridling your tongue and implementing God's wisdom to solve problems and not create them.

This is what the Lord led me to do:

*M*aking It Personal

Have you ever said something that you wish you could take back? As soon as it left your mouth, you knew it would slice into a person's heart. The words your tongue speaks can be so destructive. Work at improving your speech. Do you curse? Do you say off-color things to get a laugh? Do you belittle and intimidate others? Maybe you are the impossible person that others are praying for. Now is the time to change your heart and your speech. Read Psalm 15.

DAY 31

Discover the Real Source of Quarrels

JAMES 4:1-10

You would think that Christians would love each other and resolve conflicts easily. We should, but we don't. Christians can be arrogant and cantankerous just like everyone else when we don't submit to the Lord. James, the half-brother of Jesus, wrote his letter to get believers to act like followers of Christ, to be different from those who don't trust and abide in Him. "Put your faith into action—now!" is his message. Here is how.

Read: Pray for a receptive heart.

   A. Why do people quarrel and fight?

   B. How can you (or anyone else) change?

   C. What does "submit to God" mean?

Need: Submit yourself to God.

My greatest need today is:

God answered my prayers_____ (date) in this way:

Deed: Pray for people who quarrel with you and pick you apart. First, you submit to God. Then try to show others the value of submitting to God.

This is what the Lord led me to do:

$\mathcal{M}$aking It Personal

Submit and resist. That is the correct order. When we try in our own strength to resist the devil, we are defeated. Our pride and selfishness start arguments and cause dissention. Squabbles and pettiness result. Submit to God and humble yourself under His authority. God raises up the humble (Proverbs 3:34). Then resist Satan with the power of God. Read 1 Peter 5:8-11. Want to understand how to abide in Christ Jesus? Read John 15.

Evaluating My Progress

Now that you've completed *How to Relate to Impossible People*, it is important for you to think about what progress you have made. This will help you plan for future development.

1. Look back at the areas you chose at the beginning of the experiment under "Where to Start." Compare your initial desires with what you have done in the last month. Under each area below, circle the number on the progress scale that represents where you are now (1 = "I have made no progress"; 5 = "I have made very significant progress").

   A. Something to Understand

   Starting Point / Goal

   1 / 2 / 3 / 4 / 5

   With God's wisdom I now understand better these things:

   B. Something to Change

   Starting Point / Goal

   1 / 2 / 3 / 4 / 5

With God's strength I have changed these things:

C. Something to Accomplish

Starting Point / Goal

1 / 2 / 3 / 4 / 5

With God's courage I accomplished these things:

2. God has also helped me in other areas. These are things He has done in my life:

3. I admit it; I still need to work on these things:

4. This is what I have learned about the Lord and His greatness:

Signed_____ Date_____

The Book of Proverbs
on Relationships

"The fear of the Lord is the beginning of wisdom, and knowledge of the Holy One is understanding" (Proverbs 9:10).

The Lord is the Creator and Designer of relationships. He made people for people. But to relate with others is a challenge, as you may have discovered. People constantly change and surprise us. We change and surprise ourselves. So how can we relate with others in every circumstance?

God has the answers. Read what He says about relating to people in the book of Proverbs. It is full of wise advice. The easiest thing to do is to follow your natural instincts. But they will eventually get you into trouble. You will succeed in dealing with people when you follow closely His instructions. "There is no wisdom, no insight, no plan that can succeed against the Lord" (21:30).

Read one of these proverbs each day. Think about it throughout the day. Memorize it. Choose to practice it. Share it with others. Pray it into your life.

Avoid Big Mouths

A perverse man stirs up dissension, and a gossip separates close friends (16:28).

A fool's lips bring him strife, and his mouth invites a beating. A fool's mouth is his undoing, and his lips are a snare to his soul (18:6-7).

A gossip betrays a confidence; so avoid a man who talks too much (20:19).

Build Up People

The mouth of the righteous is a fountain of life, but violence overwhelms the mouth of the wicked (10:11).

When words are many, sin is not absent, but he who holds his tongue is wise. The tongue of the righteous is choice silver, but the heart of the wicked is of little value. The lips of the righteous nourish many, but fools die for lack of judgment (10:19-21).

The mouth of the righteous brings forth wisdom, but a perverse tongue will be cut out. The lips of the righteous know what is fitting, but the mouth of the wicked only what is perverse (10:31-32).

An anxious heart weighs a man down, but a kind word cheers him up (12:25).

A man finds joy in giving an apt reply—and how good is a timely word! (15:23).

A wise man's heart guides his mouth, and his lips promote instruction. Pleasant words are a honeycomb, sweet to the soul and healing to the bones (16:23-24).

A word aptly spoken is like apples of gold in settings of silver (25:11).

Choose Your Companions Wisely

He who walks with the wise grows wise, but a companion of fools suffers harm (13:20).

A friend loves at all times, and a brother is born for adversity (17:17).

Do not make friends with a hot-tempered man, do not associate with one easily angered, or you may learn his ways and get yourself ensnared (22:24-25).

Control Yourself

Like a city whose walls are broken down is a man who lacks self-control (25:28).

Cultivate Humility

Pride goes before destruction, a haughty spirit before a fall (16:18).

Arrogant lips are unsuited to a fool—how much worse lying lips to a ruler! (17:7).

Before his downfall a man's heart is proud, but humility comes before honor (18:12).

Who can say, "I have kept my heart pure; I am clean and without sin"? (20:9).

Haughty eyes and a proud heart, the lamp of the wicked, are sin! (21:4).

The proud and arrogant man—"Mocker" is his name; he behaves with overweening pride (21:24).

Humility and the fear of the Lord bring wealth and honor and life (22:4).

Demonstrate Patience

A prudent man keeps his knowledge to himself, but the heart of fools blurts out folly (12:23).

A patient man has great understanding, but a quick-tempered

man displays folly. A heart at peace gives life to the body, but envy rots the bones (14:29-30).

A hot-tempered man stirs up dissension, but a patient man calms a quarrel (15:18).

Better a patient man than a warrior, a man who controls his temper than one who takes a city (16:32).

He who answers before listening—that is his folly and his shame (18:13).

Through patience a ruler can be persuaded, and a gentle tongue can break a bone (25:15).

Develop Faithfulness

Love and faithfulness keep a king safe; through love his throne is made secure (20:28).

Like a bad tooth or a lame foot is reliance on the unfaithful in times of trouble (25:19).

Enjoy Life

A cheerful heart is good medicine, but a crushed spirit dries up the bones (17:22).

Forgive Genuinely

Hatred stirs up dissension, but love covers over all wrongs (10:12).

A fool shows his annoyance at once, but a prudent man overlooks an insult (12:16).

He who covers over an offense promotes love, but whoever repeats the matter separates close friends (17:9).

A man's wisdom gives him patience; it is to his glory to overlook an offense (19:11).

Grow in Knowledge

Wise men store up knowledge, but the mouth of a fool invites ruin (10:14).

With his mouth the godless destroys his neighbor, but through knowledge the righteous escape (11:9).

Whoever loves discipline loves knowledge, but he who hates correction is stupid (12:1).

The mocker seeks wisdom and finds none, but knowledge comes easily to the discerning (14:6).

The tongue of the wise commends knowledge, but the mouth of the fool gushes folly (15:2).

Gold there is, and rubies in abundance, but lips that speak knowledge are a rare jewel (20:15).

Guard Your Tongue

Whoever corrects a mocker invites insult; whoever rebukes a wicked man incurs abuse. Do not rebuke a mocker or he will hate you; rebuke a wise man and he will love you (9:7-8).

If you are wise, your wisdom will reward you; if you are a mocker, you alone will suffer (9:12).

From the fruit of his lips a man enjoys good things, but the unfaithful have a craving for violence. He who guards his lips guards his life, but he who speaks rashly will come to ruin (13:2-3).

The tongue that brings healing is a tree of life, but a deceitful tongue crushes the spirit (15:4).

The heart of the righteous weighs its answers, but the mouth of the wicked gushes evil (15:28).

Even a fool is thought wise if he keeps silent, and discerning if he holds his tongue (17:28).

Do not say, "I'll pay you back for this wrong!" Wait for the Lord, and he will deliver you (20:22).

He who guards his mouth and his tongue keeps himself from calamity (21:23).

Do not answer a fool according to his folly, or you will be like him yourself. Answer a fool according to his folly, or he will be wise in his own eyes (26:4-5).

Listen to Learn

The wise in heart accept commands, but a chattering fool comes to ruin (10:8).

A wise son heeds his father's instruction, but a mocker does not listen to rebuke (13:1).

Pride only breeds quarrels, but wisdom is found in those who take advice (13:10).

A mocker resents correction; he will not consult the wise (15:12).

Plans fail for lack of counsel, but with many advisers they succeed (15:22).

He who listens to a life-giving rebuke will be at home among the wise (15:31).

Make Honesty a Priority

A greedy man brings trouble to his family, but he who hates bribes will live (15:27).

Kings take pleasure in honest lips; they value a man who speaks the truth (16:13).

A man of perverse heart does not prosper; he whose tongue is deceitful falls into trouble (17:20).

An honest answer is like a kiss on the lips (24:26).

A lying tongue hates those it hurts, and a flattering mouth works ruin (26:28).

Manage Your Anger

A hot-tempered man must pay the penalty; if you rescue him, you will have to do it again (19:19).

Mockers stir up a city, but wise men turn away anger (29:8).

An angry man stirs up dissension, and a hot-tempered one commits many sins (29:22).

For as churning the milk produces butter, and as twisting the nose produces blood, so stirring up anger produces strife (30:33).

Please the Lord

Fools mock at making amends for sin, but goodwill is found among the upright (14:9).

To man belong the plans of the heart, but from the Lord comes the reply of the tongue (16:1).

When a man's ways are pleasing to the Lord, he makes even his enemies live at peace with him (16:7).

All a man's ways seem right to him, but the Lord weighs the heart (21:2).

When justice is done, it brings joy to the righteous but terror to evildoers (21:15).

He who pursues righteousness and love finds life, prosperity and honor (21:21).

Pursue Peace

Starting a quarrel is like breaching a dam; so drop the matter before a dispute breaks out (17:14).

He who loves a quarrel loves sin; he who builds a high gate invites destruction (17:19).

It is to a man's honor to avoid strife, but every fool is quick to quarrel (20:3).

Better to live on a corner of the roof than share a house with a quarrelsome wife (21:9).

Better to live in a desert than with a quarrelsome and ill-tempered wife (21:19).

Without wood a fire goes out; without gossip a quarrel dies down. As charcoal to embers and as wood to fire, so is a quarrelsome man for kindling strife (26:20-21).

A quarrelsome wife is like a constant dripping on a rainy day; restraining her is like restraining the wind or grasping oil with the hand (27:15-16).

Show Kindness

An evil man is trapped by his sinful talk, but a righteous man escapes trouble. From the fruit of his lips a man is filled with good things as surely as the work of his hands rewards him (12:13-14).

He who despises his neighbor sins, but blessed is he who is kind to the needy (14:21).

A gentle answer turns away wrath, but a harsh word stirs up anger (15:1).

If your enemy is hungry, give him food to eat; if he is thirsty, give him water to drink. In doing this, you will heap burning coals on his head, and the Lord will reward you (25:21-22).

Stand for Truth

Reckless words pierce like a sword, but the tongue of the wise brings healing. Truthful lips endure forever, but a lying tongue lasts only a moment (12:18-19).

The Lord detests lying lips, but he delights in men who are truthful (12:22).

The tongue has the power of life and death, and those who love it will eat its fruit (18:21).

A fortune made by a lying tongue is a fleeting vapor and a deadly snare (21:6).

A false witness will perish, and whoever listens to him will be destroyed forever (21:28).

Like a club or a sword or a sharp arrow is the man who gives false testimony against his neighbor (25:18).

Like a coating of glaze over earthenware are fervent lips with an evil heart. A malicious man disguises himself with his lips, but in his heart he harbors deceit. Though his speech is charming, do not believe him, for seven abominations fill his heart. His malice may be concealed by deception, but his wickedness will be exposed in the assembly (26:23-26).

Using This Book
with a Group

The 31-Day Experiment books have been used by groups of all kinds—home fellowship groups, church groups, Sunday school classes, women's gatherings, men's meetings, families, youth groups, new believers classes, groups preparing for missions trips, and even entire church congregations.

Doing this 31-Day Experiment together as a group has lots of benefits.

1. Everyone will be studying the same passages of Scripture each day for a month.

2. The whole group will be united in seeking to grow closer to the Lord.

3. Everyone will work on building better relationships.

4. People will share their prayer requests with the other people in the group. Everyone will grow in his or her faith as members pray for each other and experience God answering their prayers.

5. Individuals will see how the heavenly Father is working in one another's lives.

6. Members can encourage one another in their relationship with the Lord and in sharing their faith in God with other people.

Here are some guidelines for using *How to Relate to Impossible People* with your group.

Tips for the Leader

1. Prepare your lesson early, asking the Holy Spirit to give you ideas on what to teach and how to draw all the people into the discussion. Be creative. Use a variety of ways to communicate, such as videos, music, drama, and objects—whatever might be necessary to make the lessons meaningful.

2. Provide refreshments.

3. Plan the weekly meeting to last from one to one-and-a-half hours. Make sure you start and stop on time. Everyone appreciates punctuality and planning.

4. Have the group sit in a circle to enhance communication between each person.

5. Start with a group ice breaker as a way of getting to know one another a little better.

6. Encourage members to use a Bible dictionary, Bible concordance, word-study book, or online Bible study tools when they need to understand passages better.

7. Encourage people to bring their Bibles and their *How to Relate to Impossible People* books to each weekly meeting.

Group Participation Ideas

1. Remind the people of the purpose of your group and the need to deepen their relationship with the Lord.

2. Introduce the 31-Day Experiment goal—to build a habit of spending 20 to 30 minutes each day with the Lord in Bible study, prayer, and application of God's Word to life.

3. Show how the book fits into the purpose for your group. Share ideas and passages of Scripture to build each other up. Motivate the people to seek to increase their knowledge of God's Word and to pray more effectively.

Here are three of many ways to get others involved in Bible study and discussion:

Five-Week Small-Group Plan

There are 31 days of study. Do the first day together as a group with the leader showing how to do the study. Encourage group members to all start on the same day (preferably the next day) so that each person will always be on the same experiment day with the whole group. If at all possible, try to meet weekly. That way, when the next meeting occurs, the participants will have done six days of the experiment.

Plan to complete the experiment with your group in five weeks. Each week the group members should start the experiment days on the day after the group meeting. On the day of the weekly meeting, members should not do the day's experiment. Rather, they can spend that day reviewing their notes from the previous six days and thanking the Lord for all He has done in their lives.

When the group settles on the day they all want to start the experiment, send a reminder of the date, time, and place to each person. Set up a communication system so each person can share with all the others what they are learning each day and make prayer requests. Let everyone know how God answers those prayers. Encourage people to keep doing the experiment. This will help build group unity, excitement, and spiritual growth.

Be sure to read the beginning sections of this book that offer directions on how to get the most out of the study. Also, show the group the "Making It Personal" section at the end of each day with reference notes for additional information and an application project.

When you meet, discuss each day of the previous week's experiment consecutively. Ask people to share with the group what they learned and how it has affected their lives.

Begin with the whole group together, interacting on what they learned that week. If your group is large, you may want to divide into smaller subgroups, preferably with five or six people in each group. This will allow a greater number of people to share about their experiences.

Review with the group the previous week and some of the lessons they learned. What hindrances did they encounter as they sought to meet with God each day? Discuss how to discipline yourselves to overcome the hindrances in the future and how to consistently spend time with the Lord in the midst of hectic schedules.

Let everyone give input on the first day's topic before going on to the second day's topic. Encourage them to share their answers and/or questions with others in the group.

Encourage the group to share phone numbers and e-mail addresses so they can communicate with each other during the week. Motivate the people to inquire how each person is doing, answer any questions, and pray together on the phone. In this way, each person will receive several phone calls a week.

Close by briefly discussing the week ahead.

At the conclusion of each group meeting, pray together as a group, or break people into prayer partners. For the next five weeks they can be accountable to each other. Praise the Lord for all He has done, and ask Him for consistency to do the experiment faithfully each day. Pray that each person will meet with the Lord daily and will experience His presence in his or her life during the week.

Questions for Discussion

1. How did your meeting with God each day this past week go?

2. What did you have to do to set aside the 20 to 30 minutes each day?

3. What did you learn about walking with God? Loving God? Obeying God?

4. What new ideas did you get about how to relate to impossible people?

5. What happened when you tried to put some of your ideas into practice?

6. What answers to prayer did you receive? What are you still praying about?

7. What kinds of responses did you receive when you reached out to other people?

Closing

1. Celebrate all that God has done the past week and share your prayer requests for the coming week.

2. Discuss the week ahead and the passages you will be

studying. Build interest and excitement for the new things you will encounter and learn.

3. Close in group prayer. Lead in praising the Lord for His working and in asking Him to draw everyone closer to Him during the next week.

4. Encourage the people to pray earnestly for one another during the week. Remind them to phone others and send e-mails about their experiences. Empower members to share their faith with people who don't know the Lord personally.

At the End of the Experiment

1. Conclude with a special dinner or pizza. Build a fun atmosphere.

2. Make the time a celebration of completing the experiment.

3. Focus attention on the Lord and how wonderful He is.

4. Share testimonies of changed lives and healed relationships.

5. Plan for what you will do to keep growing in faith and building your group fellowship. Ask the people if they would like to do one of the other 31-Day Experiments.

6. Motivate the members to invite their friends to participate in the new experiment. Encourage them to pray for their friends so that they might join the group and get involved in growing closer to God.

Three-Week Small Group Topical Plan

You can combine certain days together by topic. Get creative! Here's just one possibility:

Week 1: Days 1–12	The Kinds of Impossible People in Our Lives
Week 2: Days 13–22	How to Relate to Impossible People (Part 1)
Week 3: Days 23–31	How to Relate to Impossible People (Part 2)

Devotional Plan for Group Meetings

For your Sunday school class or small group, *How to Relate to Impossible People* is perfectly suited for teaching and discussion. You can use one of the 31 days each meeting for a devotional thought. A different person could share each time what they learned from one of the 31 days. Another idea is to teach 31 lessons over 31 meetings.

You can shorten the number of presentations. Ask group members to share at each meeting from two, three, or more of the 31 days.

Use the book as a springboard to discussions, question-and-answer sessions, and special activities focused on the life-stage of the class you lead (such as young marrieds, career, youth, older adults, divorcees, or single parents). Emphasize personal application and life change. Pray for each other to develop better relationships with the impossible people in their lives.

Additional 31-Day Experiment Books

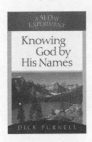

Knowing God by His Names

Our great Lord has more than 200 names! Each one puts the spotlight on a particular aspect of His infinite, rich character. This experiment gives you a different name to study each day. By learning about each name, your understanding of God will increase, and your love for our wonderful Lord will grow deeper.

Growing Closer to God

In this 31-Day Experiment, you will discover more about God's ways and perspectives. As your intimacy with God progresses, you will be transformed into the person He wants you to become.

Singles and Relationships

If you are single and want to improve your relationships, this personal devotional will be a great asset. It is not a "how to find the right person" self-help guide. Rather, it gives you biblical passages that reveal God's heart for you and the people in your life. As you journey through this 31-Day Experiment, you will understand God's instructions on how to develop good relationships in all aspects of your life—with the opposite sex, with same-sex friends, with coworkers, and with your parents and other family members.

About Dick Purnell

Dick Purnell and his wife, Paula, are on the national speakers' team for FamilyLife Marriage Conferences. He is in constant demand to speak at marriage conferences, men's retreats, single-adult events, church gatherings, and business conventions. He has spoken to audiences in all 50 states in America as well as in 12 other countries. Dick and Paula are on the full-time staff of Campus Crusade for Christ, and Dick is an adjunct professor at the Orlando Institute.

Dick is the author of 13 books. A graduate of Wheaton College, Dick holds a master of divinity degree from Trinity International University, as well as a master's degree in education specializing in counseling from Indiana University. He has been an adjunct professor at the New Life Bible College in Moscow, Russia.

Dick has been featured on many national television programs, including *The Coral Ridge Hour, The 700 Club,* and *The Nashville Hour.* He has been the main guest on many radio programs, such as *FamilyLife Today, Moody Broadcasting, Truths That Transform,* and *America's Family Counselors.* Dick's articles have appeared in many magazines, including *Decision Magazine, Worldwide Challenge,* and *Living Solo.*

Dick speaks to audiences throughout America and other countries. You can bring him to speak to your group, church, business, and convention by contacting his office at (919) 363-8000 or visiting his website at www.DickPurnell.com.